How to Let Go
A breakup recovery guide to grieving, healing & loving yourself

ANN MEADOWS

Hey love,
  Hope these two books
might help you a little ♡
The two I just powered
through just gave me so
much insight and clarity.
  Also your money from
grandparents is in these
pages.
Love you & talk to you soon,
                    mom

...s go;
...reason that they are heavy.

~Unknown

Table of Contents

INTRODUCTION

The end of a relationship can be devastating, especially when it leaves you wondering what went wrong. You keep thinking along the way that you should have known. Or perhaps you're in the position where you did know, but that doesn't make letting go any easier. It isn't easy to pick up the pieces of a shattered heart and it may leave you feeling as if you will never find love again.

You may even be afraid to try and move on for fear of having your bruised heart handed back to you, worse for wear. However this couldn't be further from the truth. In *How to Let Go: A breakup recovery guide to grieving, healing & loving yourself*, you will be shown step-by-step how to heal from heartache while learning how to find love again, starting from *within*.

The thing about a relationship is that it teaches you things. Not only about the other person, but also *about yourself*. By following the tips and strategies in this book, you will be able to look at life with a new set of eyes and walk into your future as a stronger being.

It's really true that when one door closes another opens; you need only to summon your courage and walk through the threshold.

Are you ready to take the first step? Let's begin with the first chapter.

CHAPTER 1: LET'S ALTER YOUR MINDSET

It's important to start by congratulating yourself on taking such a huge first step towards letting go of your past relationship and moving forward towards your future. Even when you know that a relationship may not have been right for you or it didn't work out as you expected, moving past a breakup is never easy. Healing your heart and healing yourself will take time, however by placing one foot in front of the other and taking it step by step you will find that you will once again experience happiness and contentment like never before. It is normal to fear change. It is like setting off into unchartered waters, but once you set sail, you have the current beneath you to carry you forward.

While letting go does not require mind-blowing magic tricks or theatrics, it will require a commitment on your part. The success of every move you make going forward will not be determined by how quickly you can get over your ex. It will be determined by the strength of the most important relationship of all; the relationship that you have with yourself.

You're intelligent enough to know that the way you think is the basis of what you feel. Do you always think that you are the one who lost because he left you? Or do you always feel that you will never find someone who is the same or even better than he was?

If you answered yes to either of those questions, it's time for you to put the boxing gloves down and stop taking jabs at your heart. Like boxers in the ring, your ability to not be defeated relies heavily on your mental game.

It's difficult to let go when you are operating from a place of loss. When you focus in on thoughts such as "I can't believe he left me" you are focusing on loss. Instinctually, you know you shouldn't do it but in reality, it's often easier to cling on to something, *anything*, than to actually accept the fact that the relationship is over. But the thing about loss is it leaves you with nothing. This is why it is so important to shift your mindset to positive thoughts that fill you and make you whole.

You have control over what you believe and ultimately feel. Your brain is the ultimate tool that can be used to help you move past your relationship. Once you alter your mindset, you alter the way you feel about the breakup.

Breaking up with your ex is tough and can leave you feeling like an emotional rollercoaster. There will be days when you feel that all the anger in the world is being stuffed inside you. Then there are days when you feel like you are within the lowest of lows because he left you. But getting hold of your thoughts and altering it to be more on the positive side is the key.

After all, you have control over what you believe and ultimately feel.

Let me explain. Have you ever heard that phrase, "Its mind over matter?"

Of course you have.

Well, the person who came up with the saying was spot on. Have you ever looked at a particular food or something that doesn't have any visual appeal, and decided you didn't like it? After a lot of encouragement from your friends, you gave in and gave it a try.

The end result? You hate it!

Of course you do.

 It feels weird on your tongue and you decide you were right in the first place. Excuse me but you already made up your mind about something before you even gave it a shot. You told your brain you didn't like the food and that was that. You controlled the response your taste buds had to the food.

Freaky, huh?

Just as you controlled the outcome of tasting the food, you control the outcome of how you will let the end of the relationship affect your life. You have the power to change how this breakup affects you. You have to decide right now that it is time to let go. It is absolutely freeing once you take that first step.

Here are some points to remember when going through a tough break up:

Just because he left you, it doesn't mean that you're not beautiful or smart or desirable. It has nothing to do with how you look and it certainly does not lessen your value as a person.

The breakup is not your punishment. Whatever wrong that you might have done before in that relationship or even the ones before that has nothing to do with what happened now. You are not being punished.

It is not your fault that you fell for him. In fact it is nobody's fault, he fell for you too, right? It just so happened that certain circumstances led your relationship to fail and it is not your fault.

If he hurt you by ending the relationship, that doesn't mean that he is a bad person. It also doesn't mean he will never find somebody to be with in the future. It just so happens that you are not the one for him. More importantly, it means that he was not the one for you.

He will definitely find someone new, and you will too. Do not be mad at his new girl, and do not make it your mission to ruin him. Remember, rash things done today might be a cause of your regret tomorrow.

Remember that it is normal to think about your breakup, you just don't want to overdo it or dwell on it. While they may not admit it out of kindness, your friends, family and coworkers will quickly tire of hearing about the failed relationship. Instead, try the 30-minute method, allow yourself to think about your ex and your breakup for a span of 30-minutes a day. Set your alarm to make sure you stop when it dings. Have something to do that will keep your mind off of him as soon as that alarm goes off.

CHAPTER 2 – WHY IS IT SO HARD TO LET GO?

Now that you understand the importance of shifting your mindset and you are ready to take the next step into the journey of letting go, there are a couple of other things you need to address. You have to determine why you are having a hard time letting go. I'll give you four common reasons why it can be hard to let go an ex. Assess what you are feeling and pinpoint the most probable one. Once you know the reason why, you can take action to move past it.

You are still mad.

Anger is a really heavy anchor that might be preventing you from moving on. If you spend every day feeling angry and focusing on how you feel about what he said or did, then you might just be sinking yourself deeper into the muck of an ended relationship.

In order to move beyond your anger, you have to accept and forgive. Accept the fact that what he did is in the past, and focus your mind on *your* future. There is absolutely nothing you can do to change it and it does not deserve your time, energy or happiness. The pain will not go away unless you forgive and let go of your anger. We will explore how to let go of this anger in a later chapter.

You are used to getting everything your way.

You can't believe he left you. You can't believe he broke up with you and broke your heart. You can't believe how he had the nerve to do it. To *you*, of all people!

Admittedly, people who are used to getting exactly what they wanted are going to struggle a bit. Those that never knew defeat are usually the ones that find it hard to move on, especially when they were the one who were left by their ex. If you are one of these people, I want you to remember how you learned to walk. You fell down, remember? No matter how much it hurt, you got back up and kept moving.

Our adult life is no different, at some point we will fall down but in picking yourself up you become stronger. Like a tiny step forward you recognize what works for you and what doesn't.

Being in denial and blind to that fact to this crucial learning curve is what is anchoring you to your pain and preventing you from letting go. Accept this as a fact of life, and when you do, you will be able to let go.

You are left with a lot of unanswered questions.

Do you feel that your break up was so sudden that it just came out of nowhere? Were you lost when he broke up with you? Maybe you felt as if you got hit by a runaway train you never saw coming. Did the anger and hurt get the better of you and you stormed off and left him or vice versa?

Relationships ending in this way are usually the ones that leave a lot of unanswered questions. Instead of talking about the problem, the couple was consumed by pain and anger that they both walk away from the "talk".

Often times, if this is the case, you will be too stuck with the questions you have to be able to fully let go.

If you can, try to have a "serious talk" with your ex, not to reconcile, but to answer some questions. If that is not possible, try answering the questions yourself. Contemplate your past relationship and see if you can answer your questions, just make sure that you don't blame yourself for everything. Once you have a good idea about why the relationship didn't last, you will be ready to head down the path of letting go.

You're ego got crushed

You may not want to admit it, but you have an ego. We all do. Sometimes our egos can be our own worst enemies. A big ego often results in somebody trying to manipulate another person or do things they normally wouldn't because their ego got a little bruised.

When a person has a big ego and they are thrust into a situation where they are humiliated or hurt, it stings. A common response is to lash out at the person who damaged the ego. The pain from the blow to the ego makes it difficult to move on and let go of the relationship.

If you feel that you are this kind of person, you have to let go of your ego first before letting go of the whole relationship. As long as you stay mad because of your crushed ego, you will not be able to move on.

Try to think of it as this, it isn't personal. It did not happen to you because you did something or didn't do something. It is just how things are, sometimes you win, and sometimes you don't get your way. Accept it and acknowledge that your ego took a little beating, but you will not let it hold you down.

Once you have determined the reason why you can't let go of your recent break up, you can concentrate on moving on.

CHAPTER 3 – LOOK FOR THE LESSON

So you've broken up with your ex whom you thought was the one. Apparently, he isn't, so gear up and get ready for when the 'real' one does comes along. Think about when you saw a fabulous pair of shoes in a store window and you knew from the moment you saw them, you had to have them. You toiled and saved until that magic day when you walked into the store and brought them home. However once you get them on your feet and took a victory lap around the living room you realize they are unbearably uncomfortable. You realize that you have learned a very important lesson; try before you buy.

Instead of dwelling on the what-ifs of your failed relationship, pause and look for the lessons that you learned. In doing so, when the next one comes along, you'll be able to use what you have learned and apply it for a more successful relationship. You don't need or deserve to take the blame for what wasn't your fault.

Here are some lessons that you can learn (the hard way) when you break up. Just like those beautiful shoes in the window, these lessons are not always fun, but they are valuable.

If he wants to cheat, he will.

This is probably the most painful lesson that any girl can learn from a relationship. To have your partner show and say that he loves you and mean it, then catching him with another girl is something so devastating that I don't wish it on anybody. But in reality, no matter how painful it is, it happens.

You are probably thinking of ways to blame yourself for his decision to cheat. Maybe you think you shouldn't have let him go to that bar with his friends so he wouldn't have met that girl. Or you should have been more supportive, more attractive, wealthier, sexier, prettier, smarter, then he wouldn't have cheated on you. You're wrong. Even if you tie your man to a leash, if he wants to cheat, he will find a way. Remember there is nothing wrong with you, he might have told you that it's your fault that he cheated, but don't believe him. It is *his* fault and *his* problem. He has a problem with his ego and so he had to prove something to himself and that's why he cheated.

You can't change him.

If you broke up with him because he was not the person you wanted him to be, you need to realize the relationship was destined to fail from the beginning. You have to stop trying to change someone or attempt to mold them into the kind of person that you want. You can't change those shoes to make them more comfortable and you can't change a man. What you can do is accept your next boyfriend for who and what he is. If he wants to change for you, he will, and he will do it on his own, without you helping him. If there are things you really cannot cope with, then don't bother getting into the relationship. You are setting yourself up for heartbreak.

Love is not enough

A relationship is a harmony of various things, not just love. In order to be successful, it has to have the right amount of communication, understanding and compromise, which will ultimately lead to a strong love for one another.

Being single is not that bad.

After your breakup, you might find it hard to regain your feet because you got so used to doing everything with your ex. Now is the time to explore and rekindle relationships with your family and friends. Learn to do things on your own. When you think about it, being single is actually a good thing. You can go wherever you want without worrying about asking permission or thinking that you can't do this or that because your partner doesn't want you to. Now is actually the time to spend time on yourself. You'll be amazed how happy you'll be without him.

Now you know the lesson that your break up taught you. It is now up to you to apply what you have learned to your next relationship. You can also apply the lesson you learned to the process of letting go. You will feel more confident in your decisions and responses as you continue to move forward.

Whenever a thought or a conversation makes you mad or makes you want to cry, remember the lessons you have learned and shift what you are feeling into a more positive light.

CHAPTER 4 – GRIEVE FOR THE BETTER YOU

Grieving is a normal part of life. It is normal to grieve or mourn if we lost somebody or we experience something sad or painful.

With that said, it is important, that while you are living through the aftermath of your breakup, we don't want to skip over the grieving process. You need to grieve or all those feelings will sneak up on you when you are least prepared for them. You need to deal with it now.

For some people, they think that recovering from a break up is as easy as a snap of a finger. They think that when they take you to a bar to drink and meet some eligible bachelor that you will be just peachy the next day. Unfortunately, that isn't the case. In fact, it is better if you stick with the process of grief and not skip over it all in favor of ignoring it ever happened. Instead, put a rain check on your friends' bar hopping escapades for now. Take time to recover from the break up.

Here are the 5 steps of grief that everyone going through the same situation as you will follow. You can take time with each step, and make sure you understand that there is no hurrying this process. There is no predetermined amount of time to grieve.

Denial

This is the part where the initial shock of the breakup plays its part. The minute you hear your guy leaving, or breaking up with you, you will not immediately believe it. It will simply not sink in.

Give your mind a chance to catch up with what happened. Take a few deep breaths and process the words and actions while giving your brain the chance to let it sink in. Denial is essentially a safety net. It gives you the chance to work through the situation without feeling too deeply until you are ready to process the emotions. Don't diminish your relationship or pretend it never happened as part of the denial phase. Don't try and continue the numbness denial brings by imbibing too much or using drugs. Let it run its course.

Anger

You can say that you are on this stage when you are mad at your ex for making you go through what you are going through right now. In the previous stage, you were not feeling anger because you were still taking it all in. You weren't feeling much of anything in that initial phase. Now that all the denial has faded, you are mad as heck!

Don't worry, it is ok to feel angry and it is a natural process that you have to get through. Control your anger and do not do anything that will make your grief worse, like doing something illegal. Always keep your anger in check.

The best and quickest way to get beyond this stage is to release that anger in a constructive manner.

The first thing you are going to want to do is either open up a blank document on your laptop or grab a pencil and paper.

Begin by addressing the letter to your ex. Why are you writing a letter? It's hard to be honest with others and even harder to be honest with ourselves. However a private letter gives us a safe place to let out our emotions and express the things that we never had a chance or the courage to say.

Start the letter by letting out all the thoughts and emotions that are currently inside of you. Write out your frustrations, write out your fears about the relationship, write out why are upset.

Do you want to scream at him? Write it out.

Are you confused? Write it out.

Does he make you feel like crying when you think about him? Write it out.

Again, be very honest with yourself here because in order to heal you have to get remove the bad things in order to clean the wound.

Next, in the same letter write down everything that you learned as a result of your relationship with him. Not just the things you learned to avoid but also the things you learned about *yourself*. List out as many lessons that come to mind.

Finally, end the letter by thanking him for the lessons that the relationship enabled you to learn. In your own words, tell him that you forgive him for any hurt that he has caused you. Wish him the best and acknowledge to him that you are letting him go and moving forward with your life.

Once the letter is complete, read it aloud to yourself.

Read it with all the emotions that have been residing within you and feel each one being released with each word. You may find it difficult getting through the letter and that's okay. Keep reading it until you can read the letter in a clear, strong voice. As you read it through the final time, acknowledge the words and their meaning. Let it resound not only in your ears but also in your heart.

After reading the letter, delete it. Or if you wrote it, rip up the letter and throw it away.

This is very important because this is you letting go and releasing the hold that your unexpressed emotions had on you.

Then, take a deep breath and relax. Releasing emotions is never an easy task, so be sure to reward yourself for taking such a big step to heal.

Other Ideas to Release Negative Energy

Go for a hike, get on the treadmill or scrub your kitchen from top to bottom. Release all that energy you have that is fueled by your anger. It also helps to talk it out with a good friend. Acknowledge the anger, release it and move forward into your new life.

Bargaining

Now, that you are no longer angry, you are probably thinking, "Hey, wait, I want you and I will do whatever it takes to be with you." You long for those moments in the relationship when everything seemed so great and are ready to bargain with him to get those moments back.

Your willingness to sacrifice and change just to get him back is now obvious. You might even come to a point when you are willing to forget all that he has done in order to get him back. You must hold on, I know I told you that this is a stage that you have to encounter, but this doesn't mean that you can get on your knees and beg him to love you again. It does not work that way. You can certainly change those things about you that maybe he said he didn't like, but do it for you—not him.

The changes you were willing to make for him can be used as a tool to help you through this stage of grief. Maybe you promised to get in better shape. That is an excellent goal but ensure you are doing it so *you* feel better. Join a gym and go for it. Consider taking up a hobby that will make you feel more fulfilled. It is all about you and your own health and wellbeing. Make a bargain with *yourself* to feel better.

Depression

Now comes the sad part. When all the anger fades away, and all your bargaining ideas are shunned, what will you be left with? I know you answered, "Nothing." While that isn't the least bit true, you won't immediately believe it and will inevitably begin the depression phase.

Don't force yourself to go out and mingle with other people just to "look ok" when you are crumbling inside. Whoever said that locking yourself up in your room is a bad idea doesn't know what he is talking about. Go ahead, isolate yourself from people and spend some time alone. It is ok to cry. Just don't spend years inside your room, and make sure you take care of yourself through the process.

Although this is probably the most miserable stage of grief, it is a part of the healing process. The best thing you can do is acknowledge the loss and the feelings associated with it and keep moving forward. Do your best to maintain normal routines and eventually, you will heal and move on to the final stage of grief.

Acceptance

This is what you are aiming for. When you have finally realized that you are only hurting yourself while you are skulking in your room while your ex is out there enjoying his life and being seen in every bar and dancing with every woman he meets, then it is time to get out and enjoy your single life.

It is important that during this time you focus solely on improving yourself and not your ex. Why? Because when he gets tired of his nightly party and he spends his nights alone in his room, that's when he will realize what he lost. You chose to take your time getting through the process and coming out on the other side a healthy person once again. He, however, is going to be bombarded with those feelings because he ignored them. So when he calls and asks you to reconcile, you won't be there. You will be somewhere, enjoying your single life and not caring about him.

Acceptance doesn't mean you like what happened, but you have realized it is what it is. Your life is going on just fine without him. You are not thinking about him or what he did every moment of the day. Maintaining routines and enjoying life is the best way to reach acceptance. Live your life for *you* and fall in love with the new, stronger woman whom you have become.

CHAPTER 5 – FIND LOVE IN YOURSELF

Have you heard that saying you have to love yourself in order to be loved?

Another great saying.

You have to love yourself enough to demand you are treated the way you deserve.

Before you read further, I would like for you to read one of my favorite inner beauty affirmations taken from *The Seeds of Beauty: Defining Your Beauty & Style from the Inside Out* by Lakeysha-Marie Green. Print it out and let it serve as a reminder of the relationship that you must continually develop within as you navigate through the healing process. By making the commitment to acknowledge the beauty and strength within yourself, you are already taking one of the most important steps towards a more fulfilling and nurturing life.

[Your name],

To you, I will never be a fair-weather friend.

When you are afraid,

I will give you the courage to step forward.

If ever you make a mistake,

I will never lose faith in you.

And when you begin to doubt how

beautiful you are, I will remind you.

Today and every day

I promise to always stand by you.

You are me. I am you.

I love you.

After the breakup, did you walk to a mirror and pick out every flaw you thought you could see? Did you think you were somehow not worthy of his love? It is absolutely crucial you have a healthy self-esteem before you jump into another relationship. Insanity is doing the same thing over and over and expecting a different outcome.

You need to take a step back and find love in yourself before you attempt to gain another's love. One of the quickest ways to achieve a healthier self-esteem is by committing to using positive affirmations every single day. The following statements are an example of what you could use, but certainly tweak it to suit you.

I have pretty eyes

I love my sense of style

I like that my hair is naturally curly

I have a nice, healthy figure

I am a confident person

I am worthy of love

I am really good at my job

Now, walk back to that mirror and identify five things you like about yourself. They can be some of the examples from above or things you can see in your mirror. It doesn't matter what it is, *find it.* It's true that you teach others how to treat you by the way you treat them but more importantly, you teach others how to treat you by the way *you treat yourself.* If you fail to see the beautiful within yourself and put yourself down, you may soon find others doing the same.

Now that you have those five things, look into the mirror and say them like you mean it. Do this every single day before you walk out the door. When you are feeling a little shaky or down on yourself, get your bum up and give yourself a pep talk! Tell yourself the words that you need to hear. Never forget that real love begins with you.

These tips along with the positive affirmation mentioned above are meant to make you feel better and make you see your worth and ultimately help nourish your self-love.

Get plenty of sleep

I know that ever since your break up day, you haven't had enough sleep. So the first thing that I want you to do is to replenish your energy levels by getting plenty of sleep. Your physical and mental health depend on you getting adequate sleep. You will look better and feel better.

Exercise

When I say exercise, I don't mean the rigorous training exercise that health buffs do. Just a simple jogging or brisk walk around the park will do. Why? Because when you exercise, it takes your mind away from your break up, and it literally makes you feel good, and a bonus is that it can make you look good too.

Have a Makeover

You can cut or color your hair to welcome the new you and revamp your wardrobe. Doing so will separate you from your past self; you will be able to psychologically start a new life, without your ex around you. You don't have to spend a fortune; you just do what you think will make you feel different and confident to face and enjoy the world alone.

Pamper yourself

Get your nails done, have a foot spa, or a full body massage. You can even go on a vacation alone or with your family. Do anything that makes you feel better. Doing so will help you be more in tuned with yourself.

Rally up your friends

If you are one of those girls who tend to lose time with their friends when they have a boyfriend, you need to rekindle those friendships. After you have done all the previous steps and you are ready to embrace your single self, call up your friends and set up a night out. Enjoy yourselves and party the night away. If you are not the type that is into nights out, then head to the mall and spend the day with your friends, who knows, the one for you might just be there too.

CHAPTER 6 – BE OPEN TO LOVE AGAIN

I know that the idea of being in love again and having another person care for you may not be on your mind right now. But you have to remember that you can't close your door forever. There will come a time when a new man will come along, usually when you least expect it. Your next trip to the grocery store may end up in a love match in the produce section. A day at the park with your dog could end up leading you to the man who will give you a happy ever after. Roll your eyes, but it does happen.

If you are feeling a little gun shy about a relationship right now, it is okay. Eventually you'll get to that point, and when you finally do, only you will know if you are ready.

Here are some questions that you will need to answer truthfully to determine if you are indeed ready for a new love or not.

If your ex calls you up and begs you to get back with him, will you say no without having second thoughts?

Once you have second thoughts if you really want to move on or you want to get back with your ex, then that's the number one sign that you are not ready yet.

Can you get through an entire conversation without bringing up stories about your ex?

If conversations that you have with others still end up being about your ex in one way or another, you are not quite ready.

If you are talking to someone and your ex is brought up, can you respond without being angry or crying?

When thoughts of your ex still bring tears to your eyes or still lead to an ugly bout with the one who brought it up, then that is a sure fire way that you are still hanging on to your relationship baggage. Spending time healing *you* is better than looking for a new love at the moment.

Can you think of your past relationship with a positive outlook? Can you focus on the lessons instead of the pain?

When you can focus on what your relationship taught you instead of how it hurt you and made you miserable, then you can be sure that you are ready to meet someone new. The old baggage is gone and you are a brand new woman ready for love.

I hope you have answered all the questions truthfully; it's ok if you are not ready yet. We all are different and we all went through different challenges in life. So if according to the questions, you are not quite ready, then you can go back to spending time with yourself. Healing takes time and maybe you still need more.

It is crucial you give yourself time to completely heal from the pain of your defunct relationship. Getting involved with another person too soon will not allow you to blossom and grow as an individual. You are likely to be a little insecure following the end of a relationship. There is a good chance you will bring those insecurities into your new relationship. You would be inadvertently sabotaging any chance at finding love again.

You deserve better for yourself. Period.

Imagine working out at the gym and getting all sweaty and then crawling into a bed with clean sheets. You are sullying them right out of the gate. Bringing your baggage from your previous relationship will not give you the chance to truly start fresh.

If on the other hand you answered 'yes' to all the above questions, then that is a sign that you are indeed ready to meet someone new. Be open to possibilities and do not close your doors to anyone. Keeping your door open is a huge help not only to make sure you find your new love, but also to make sure that you are living your life the way you should live it and enjoying every moment. Happiness takes many forms but the one constant in life is that happiness is beautiful.

CHAPTER 7 – VISUALIZE YOUR NEXT RELATIONSHIP

Now that you are open to loving again, you want to ensure you don't go rushing into a relationship with the first guy you meet. Sounds obvious, right? But trust me, we've all been there. You see that guy across the room, your eyes meet, your heart kicks up a beat and you just know he is the one. But is he really or he is your rebound guy?

So how will you make sure that you don't end up in a rebound relationship or a relationship where you will be disappointed and it will crumble sooner or later? The key is to visualize what you want. It doesn't mean that you have to be choosy in picking your next relationship. You won't visualize things like you want a handsome, rich, sweet and perfect guy. It does not work that way. Visualizing that way will only make you drive away every potential guy just because they are not perfect. You don't want to set a standard so high that nobody will ever measure up. Nobody is perfect. Visualize the *ideal* man rather than the *perfect* man.

Here are a few tips on how to visualize your next relationship:

Create a vision board or vision notebook

Go to your local bookstore and buy a cork board or notebook. Now if you chance upon a picture of a happy couple in a magazine cut it out and pin it to your board. Maybe the couple has a certain glow about them that is undeniably happiness at its best. If the look makes you feel all warm and fuzzy, pin it to your board. It can be a picture of a happy family, a couple having dinner, a couple walking in the park, or some delicious food. Yes! It can be food; if you like the food and you dream about eating that particular food with your main squeeze, it deserves getting pinned to your board. Imagine eating chocolate covered strawberries or feeding each other plump grapes. Your vision board can consist of anything at all, as long as it gives out positive energy when you see it.

Redecorate with positive symbols

Redecorate your room with colors, photos or objects that inspire you. You can even download inspirational wallpaper apps onto your phone. Seeing a lot of things that are meaningful to you can have a positive effect on you and your acceptance that there is love out there, you just haven't met him yet.

Be Consistent

Having a vision board and decorating your room or workspace with Aphrodite will be useless if you don't spend any time actually looking at it. Your brain needs consistency in order to really program it for love or anything else. Make it a point to look at your vision board a few minutes every morning before you start preparing for school or work. It helps to set the mood for the day and will subconsciously gear you for love the moment you head out the door.

Be Patient

Don't get too hasty and make it your life mission to find a man. It needs to happen naturally. Not every guy you encounter should be seen as a potential mate. Visualizing doesn't necessarily mean your dream man is going to fall in your lap the next day. These things take time. Just be patient and know that it is coming. Instead of spending your time waiting for someone to fall in love with you, focus instead on falling in love with yourself. Rediscover your likes & dislikes, give time to others, challenge yourself with new opportunities.

Have Faith

This does not require you to be religious or perform rituals. You just have to believe that your next relationship is going to come and when it does, you have to be ready for it.

As you go through this exercise, it's important to visualize what you want to feel, like extreme love, overflowing happiness, peace of mind; whatever a healthy relationship looks like to you. Really take the time to discern how you feel and identify the core values that will bring you fulfillment in your next relationship.

CONCLUSION

You suffered a blow when your relationship ended, there is no disputing that. However, now is time to let go and discover how exceptional life can be when you pull yourself up and out of the void of the past and redirect your focus to your future. Never forget your value and never second guess your worth. Love yourself enough to find the right man who will love you the way you deserve and desire.

Relationships end. That is a fact of life we all must endure. However, the end of a relationship should never be the end of *you*. Let it serve its purpose as a stepping stone on your path to emerging a stronger, wiser and more beautiful person.

###

Thank you for reading my book. If you enjoyed it, won't you please take a moment to leave me a review at your favorite retailer?

Thanks!

Ann Meadows

PREVIEW "WHY DID I DO THAT? HOW TO BEAT THE CYCLE OF INSECURITY & JEALOUSY IN YOUR RELATIONSHIP"

Elizabeth Bowen, an Irish writer, once said that "Jealousy is no more than feeling alone against smiling enemies." It was such an eloquent way to describe a frustrating and ugly emotion.

At the root of it all, jealousy is an emotion that is rooted in fear, concern, and anxiety over the perception that you may lose something that has a lot of personal value to you.

The beautiful and flirtatious coworker. The female best friend that "knows him better than you do". The ex-girlfriend. These people that we consider to be threats often aren't but that doesn't mean that we can't control our suspicions. Even the most trustworthy of couples can feel twinges of jealousy every now and then.

Jealousy can take control of our lives – and quickly too. It is a wicked emotion but one that we can control. The feeling of helplessness that sweeps over us when we get jealous over something or someone can be incredibly debilitating.

What Is The Point Of Jealousy?

The truth is that a little bit of jealousy is perfectly natural. When you feel that twinge of jealousy, what you are really feeling is a fear that your significant other might leave you or feel a stronger connection with someone else. You're afraid you might lose him. That, in and of itself, is quite normal. We can get territorial; it's natural.

Scientists believe that this type of jealousy is in fact, a biological imperative (in other words, it's a part of human nature). It is instinctual to look for the best reproductive partner, even if the exact definition of that differs among all of us. The act of jealousy may just be an internal mechanism to ensure access to the best partner for us.

However, it starts to venture into dangerous territory when you start to act on those feelings in an inappropriate way or if you don't convey those feelings to him in a healthy manner. Bottling your jealousy up can make it grow and fester – like a wound that isn't healing properly. You don't want that jealousy to turn into gangrene.

What Will This Book Cover?

In between these pages, you'll find a lot of information about jealousy and insecurity. Not only that, you will find out what is healthy and what isn't, and how these two emotions can completely destroy a relationship.

I will also delve into what it would be like to be on the other end of jealousy (if your significant other is jealous of you) and what can be done about that situation.

Other topics that will be covered are:

Different forms of jealousy

The difference between jealousy and insecurity

How to overcome jealousy

How to save a relationship riddled with jealousy

Jealousy doesn't have to ruin your relationship as long as you are willing to try some of the steps in this book.

CHAPTER 1: SIGNS OF INSECURITY & JEALOUSY AND WHY TOO MUCH IS A PROBLEM

Let's Talk About Insecurity For A Moment...

Insecurity is a lack of confidence or assurance. You can also call it self-doubt, anxiety, or a lack of confidence. If you are feeling insecure, there is more of a chance that you will develop unhealthy levels of jealousy while you are in a relationship.

How Can You Tell If Someone Is Being Insecure?

There are many different types of people and we all handle our insecurities in different ways. We can categorize most people into six different categories based on how they handle what they view to be their shortcomings:

People who take those insecurities as a challenge (to better themselves so that they can overcome them),

People that use humor as a defense mechanism,

People who just surround themselves with positivity and pretend that they don't have any insecurities at all,

People who lie about themselves in order to cover up any insecurities (I mean, wild outlandish tales!),

People who verbally doubt themselves and put themselves down, and

People who act out because of their insecurities in order to cover them up.

Most of us strive for the first category but end up falling into one of the latter ones. That doesn't mean that we can't change though.

Below, I've listed 15 ways that you can tell if someone is acting a certain way because he or she is insecure. Look at your behavior and look at the behavior of your significant other. If you recognize some of these behaviors within yourself, it might be time to change.

Overly Critical About Others.

If you are overly critical of others, it might be because you are secretly comparing yourself with them. It isn't healthy to be constantly comparing yourself to others. If someone is insecure about their looks, they'll point out how ugly they think other people are or will point out someone else's flaws.

There Is A Lot Of Bragging Going On.

If someone is feeling insecure, they could try to hide them by exaggerating about their successes. It is not bad to be proud of your work or success. However, there is a difference between feeling proud and bragging. When you are confident or proud of an accomplishment, you don't have the intention of belittling others to make you or other people feel better. Bragging is when you want others to pat you on the back or feel bad about their lack of accomplishments.

They Are Not Supportive Of Your Successes.

Some people who are insecure feel the need to put others down. Some do this overtly (like the people who point out other people's flaws) while others do so quietly, by not being supportive.

In the beginning of my current relationship, we got off to a bit of a rocky start. We both quit our jobs so that we could take care of his grandfather. It was tough on him because he had to see his grandfather in a new light and he had to take care of him physically. I came with him as extra support (moral support and physical support – extra hands are always helpful).

We soon got word that one of his family members was going to be taking our places so we began to look toward our futures. I got online and quickly found a great job that allowed me to work remotely – which meant that I could start immediately. It was for something that I felt passionate about: writing. Unfortunately, instead of being supportive and happy for me, he put down my new job and was not as supportive as I would have hoped.

With the stresses of his grandfather's condition, the big move back home (we had to move out of state to help his family), and the pressure of starting new when we got home, I felt as though I should cut him some slack. We sat down one night and talked about his behavior and our situation.

He admitted his jealousy that I got a job in the field I wanted rather quickly. I assured him of his success and told him that I would help him find his passion so he would be as happy as I was. I wanted him to succeed. I didn't want to brag about my job, nor did I want to belittle him because he didn't have a passion.

Our openness with each other and our thoughtfulness toward each other, paired with our love and our honesty (especially about our stubbornness) has proved to get us through the toughest times. We're now happily married and we both work toward our passions: me with my love of words and him with his love of the outdoors.

Gossip, Gossip, Gossip.

Everyone has been guilty of gossip at one time or another. It's not just a woman's trait either. Guys gossip just as much, though not often as overtly as we do. However, if you're gossiping about someone's shortfalls or shortcomings in order to feel better about yourself, you're not doing anyone any favors.

Gossiping can be an extremely vengeful act. It has been proven time and time again that words are just as impactful if not worse than physical blows.

Name-Calling In Intense Situations.

If you ever get in a debate with someone who is insecure, you may find that they can be prone to name-calling especially in overly stressful or intense situations. This is a horrible way of dealing with stress and for some, it can be the last resort. People who are confident in themselves and their point of view don't often turn to name-calling, even in intense situations.

They Keep Bringing Up Past Mistakes Of Yours.

If someone is focused on making you feel bad in order to lift themselves up, it's most likely due to their insecurities. We've all made mistakes in the past and we're all going to make mistakes in the future. What gets us through that is being honest and learning from those mistakes.

If you've learned from it but your significant other keeps bringing it up anyway, it's time for them to look inwards at themselves.

They Take Everything Personally.

When we take something too personal, it is because we are feeling guilty or insecure about something. For example, I belong to a few critique groups. When we are in meetings, we normally pass our work around and someone reads it out loud. After which the members of the group take turns talking about where we can improve and why.

We premise each meeting by encouraging constructive criticism and by strongly emphasizing the fact that these are merely suggestions and that we don't have to use them if we don't want to. Despite all of that premise, we do have the occasional slip-up where someone isn't being constructive or someone takes the criticism as a personal attack on themselves. As writers, we know how vulnerable we can be during this time.

When you are in a relationship, it can feel like you're always in a critique group. If you are in a healthy relationship with yourself and with your significant other, this should be a good thing. The purpose of critique groups is to help each other be better writers. If we all walked on eggshells with each other instead of giving each other critiques, it would be the equivalent to letting each other walk around with our zippers down. We want each other to succeed. We want the best for each other.

It should be the same with you and your partner. You should want each other to succeed.

Belittling Someone Else's Success.

Some people will try to prove why other people's successes aren't actual successes or aren't earned in order to feel better about themselves.

People who have a healthy relationship with themselves and with others will use other people's successes to inspire themselves and help push themselves. These successes are appreciated and are something to be proud of.

When They Are Called Out On That Behavior, They Make Excuses.

People who are confident in themselves know that it is important to be able to hold ourselves accountable to our own actions. If someone calls us out on our inappropriate behavior, we should own up to it. That being said, it doesn't normally go smoothly like this:

"You're being a jerk."

"Wh... Yeah, you're right. I'm sorry. I just feel..."

…but it should. Of course, it would probably help if you didn't use words like "jerk". This is where "I statements" come into play. It should really go like this:

"I felt hurt by what you just said."

"I'm sorry. I didn't mean to hurt you."

There; that's better.

They Are A Poor Sport When They Lose Or A Horrid Winner When They Win.

Some people feel like they have to win all the time. It's the only time that they feel validated- when they are getting praise for being the best. This shows an incredible amount of insecurity.

My husband and I will be the first people to tell you that we are competitive. We're big into board gaming so we know what it is like to win and to lose and we try our best at doing both with grace. It didn't used to be that way though.

While I have always tried to be an unobtrusive winner, I used to be a horrible loser. If I wasn't winning or actively helping my team win, I felt useless. Feeling useless was something that I used to struggle with. So feeling this way with my close friends brought out ugly feelings and a big, nasty, pouty lip. That being said, I have since learned how to gracefully lose (believe me, it took a lot of practice and a lot of perspective).

They Can Attach The World's Negativity To People That They Don't Like.

If someone is insecure and they don't like someone, suddenly everything that goes wrong is that person's fault. They caused the coffee machine to break. They caused this person's inability to meet a deadline. They are the reason why everything is going wrong.

People who are insecure have a tendency of trying to put down the people around them. It doesn't always happen; but when it does, it's to help them with their own self-esteem. The problem is that it never really works. Why would "putting someone else down" help "lift you up?"

Degrade People That They Are Close To Or Have Lost Touch With.

Just like gossip, some people who are insecure find it necessary to publicly shame or bad-mouth others so that they will feel better. If someone is doing this, it may be because they don't want you to look toward them due to their anxieties.

People who are confident in themselves don't have to speak ill of those that they have lost friendships or relationships with in the past. For them, the past is often left in the past and they may look back at their past relationships for two things: (1) the lessons that they have learned, and (2) fond memories. Why look in the past negatively? What will that accomplish?

They Hate Rich People.

This is an example of disliking people because of their success. Sure, for the privileged and the rich, things may appear to come easy but that shouldn't affect how you live your life. You make your own decisions about how you live your life and they will do the same with their lives.

They Encourage You To Stop Doing Things When The Going Gets Tough.

If you give up, it makes them feel better about not trying as hard. I've seen it happen firsthand and it was both of our faults. When I was starting out in the writing field, I had a few friends who were less than supportive. Sometimes, I would go out and seek some support from them (my fault because I was really trying to lift myself up).

When I had put myself in a difficult situation, some of my friends would say, "Just give up. Seriously. It'd be so much easier to go out and get a 9 – 5." Deep down, I knew that was right but I also knew that it wasn't the right path for me. Writing wasn't my life. I lived my life. But writing was my passion and I knew better than to give it up.

ANN MEADOWS

It soon came out that those people were having issues with their personal and professional lives. They finally came out and told me that I make "following your passion" look too easy and they hated me for it. Telling me to give up was easier than trying to follow their passions.

They Have A Tendency To Be Pessimistic.

Insecure people are often pessimistic. It has to do with their view of the world. If something isn't perfect, then it is wrong. They view themselves this way also. Since they aren't perfect, there are things that are wrong about them. It is a very distorted and a "black and white" way to view things.

So What Does Any Of That Have To Do With Jealousy?

Jealousy is an emotion that is often caused my insecurities with the relationship and with yourself. If you don't feel good about yourself, you may start to think that your significant other feels the same way about you. When you start to doubt his love and confidence in you, there is more of a chance that you'll think he'll start to look elsewhere to fill his needs and desires.

Not only that, there are different types of jealousy as well. When you are referring to jealousy within a relationship, you are often talking about what scientists call **sexual jealousy**. That happens when a person's significant other displays possible sexual interest in someone else. It's even more powerful if you suspect that your significant other has already been involved in infidelity.

Scientifically speaking, when you talk about the different types of sexual jealousy between men and women, scientists are more apt to say that women have a tendency to worry more about **emotional infidelity** and fear of abandonment over sexual infidelity. If you think that your significant other is emotionally connecting with someone else, you start to get jealous. Your guy won't realize why though since he hasn't physically or sexually cheated on you. This difference has to do with how we are wired.

Unfortunately, our difference in wiring is also the reason why we can't effectively communicate with one another also. It's similar to trying to talk to someone who speaks a different language. Some things can get through but the more subtle and specific things get lost in translation.

How Insecurity and Jealousy Interact

Insecurity will breed jealousy. Think of the different types of jealous thoughts that you've had in the past. Have you recognized a few jealous thoughts about your significant other before? Think about that particular jealous thought and the thoughts that came after that. An ugly criticism or question can quickly turn to an inner criticism about yourself.

"What would he ever see in her? Maybe it's because she's so much prettier than me…"

These thoughts and criticisms about yourself are even more dangerous than your perceived threat! When you are insecure, you begin to question your significant other's thoughts, intentions, actions, and words, instead of trusting him.

The Role That Technology Plays

The advancements in technology over the past few years is fantastic. We are able to do almost everything with a small "magic box" that fits in our pockets. However, this is also one of the reasons that we can feel insecure and jealous. Technology can breed deception between the strongest of couples. Texting, e-mail, social media, messaging. All of these things are ways that we can reach out and communicate with others. As those lines of communication open, we can become suspicious of each other's motives.

"Is that text message from her again?"

"Why did your ex send you that picture?"

"Did she drunk dial you? AGAIN?"

These instances make us feel insecure about ourselves and how attracted your significant other is to these other women.

What Happens If You Have Unhealthy Levels Of Jealousy In Your Relationship?

When jealousy is unhealthy, it can cause the demise of your relationship. It might sound a bit melodramatic to put it that way but, hey, aren't you being a little melodramatic when you act overly jealous? I know I do.

However, it doesn't mean that your relationship is over. You can get through it. The process involves a lot of communication and a lot of trust. That can and will be difficult for both of you but you both have to believe in the relationship and yourselves in order to get through it. Let's begin by tackling the root causes.

###

I hope you were able to take a little something away from this preview that can help you in your own life. Should you wish to continue reading this book or explore my other books, just turn the page.

EXPLORE OTHER BOOKS BY THIS AUTHOR

Below you'll find some of my other popular books.

Why Did I Do That? How to beat the cycle of insecurity & jealousy in your relationship

Are You...You? 10 signs you're sacrificing too much in a relationship and what to do about it now.

Love Knows No Bounds: A woman's guide to a healthy long distance relationship

ABOUT THE AUTHOR

Inspired by her own capricious journey to finding love, Ann Meadows began writing to show readers how to plant seeds of unconditional love within themselves that transpire into fulfilling relationships. Drawing from her personal experiences Ann tackles cringe-worthy dating pitfalls to pesky emotional hangovers. She is an avid foodie, passionate writer and lives to see her readers shine.

Made in the USA
San Bernardino, CA
17 June 2019